I0816323

This revised version was first published
in 2025 by Hungry Tomato Ltd
F15, Old Bakery Studios,
Blewetts Wharf, Malpas Road
Truro, Cornwall, TR1 1QH, UK

A CIP catalog record for this book is available from the British Library.

Beetle Books is an imprint of Hungry Tomato.

ISBN 9781835690987

Printed and bound in China

Discover more at:
www.hungrytomato.com

ANIMAL HABITATS

Annabel Griffin

Illustrated by Rose Maclachlan

CONTENTS

Words in **bold** can be found in the glossary.

WHO'S HIDING?

Can you spot these animals?

pages 40-55

IN THE OCEANS AND SEAS

There is so much to see in our oceans and seas! Can you spot the amazing underwater creatures that make their homes here?

HERE COME THE SHARKS!

A shark is a type of fish. There are over 500 different kinds of shark! These are just a few of them.

Killing machines

Great whites are deadly **predators** but it's very rare for them to attack humans.

Gentle giants

Whale sharks are the biggest fish in the sea and can live to be 150 years old!

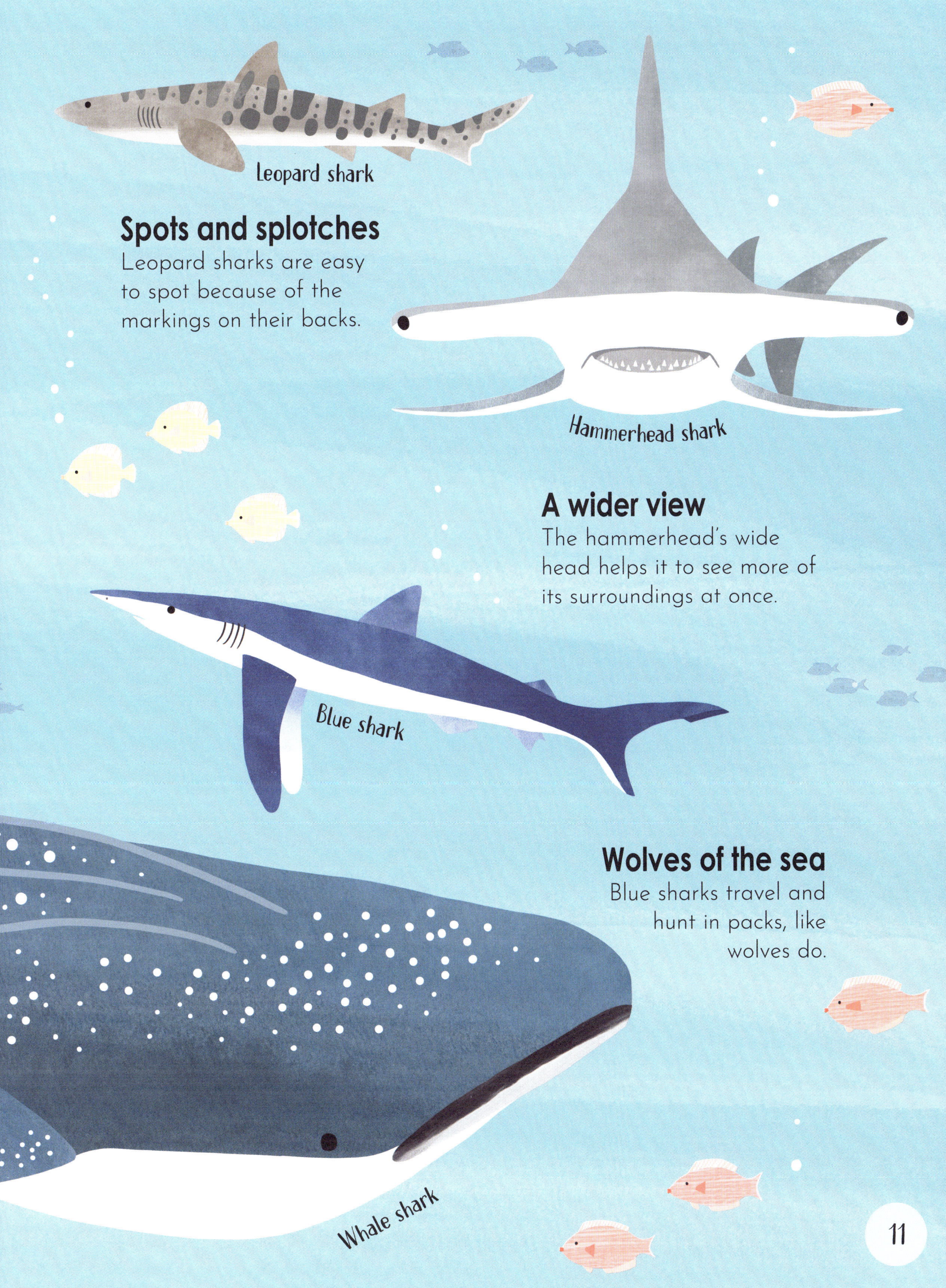

Spots and splotches

Leopard sharks are easy to spot because of the markings on their backs.

A wider view

The hammerhead's wide head helps it to see more of its surroundings at once.

Wolves of the sea

Blue sharks travel and hunt in packs, like wolves do.

LIFE ON THE REEF

Coral reefs are large underwater structures made of coral. They are home to thousands of sea creatures!

Slithery swimmers

Sea snakes are some of the deadliest snakes in the world.

An unusual friendship

Sea anemones have poisonous stinging tentacles to catch fish but...

...clownfish are **immune** to their sting. They make anemones their home and help to attract other fish for them to eat.

Here for the food!

Hawksbill turtles love to eat sponges found on reefs.

Sea fans are a type of coral.

Plant or animal?

Coral, sponges, anemones, and urchins may look like weird plants, but they are actually all animals!

WEIRD AND WONDERFUL FISH

There are some very strange looking fish in the ocean! Some of them have special skills too.

Big and brainy

Manta rays are the largest rays in the world and have the biggest brains of any fish. That's smart!

Manta ray

All puffed up

When they get scared, pufferfish **inflate** to several times their normal size; like a water balloon.

Pufferfish

World's fastest fish

Sailfish are one of the fastest fish in the ocean, and are thought to reach speeds of up to 68 miles per hour (109 km/h)!

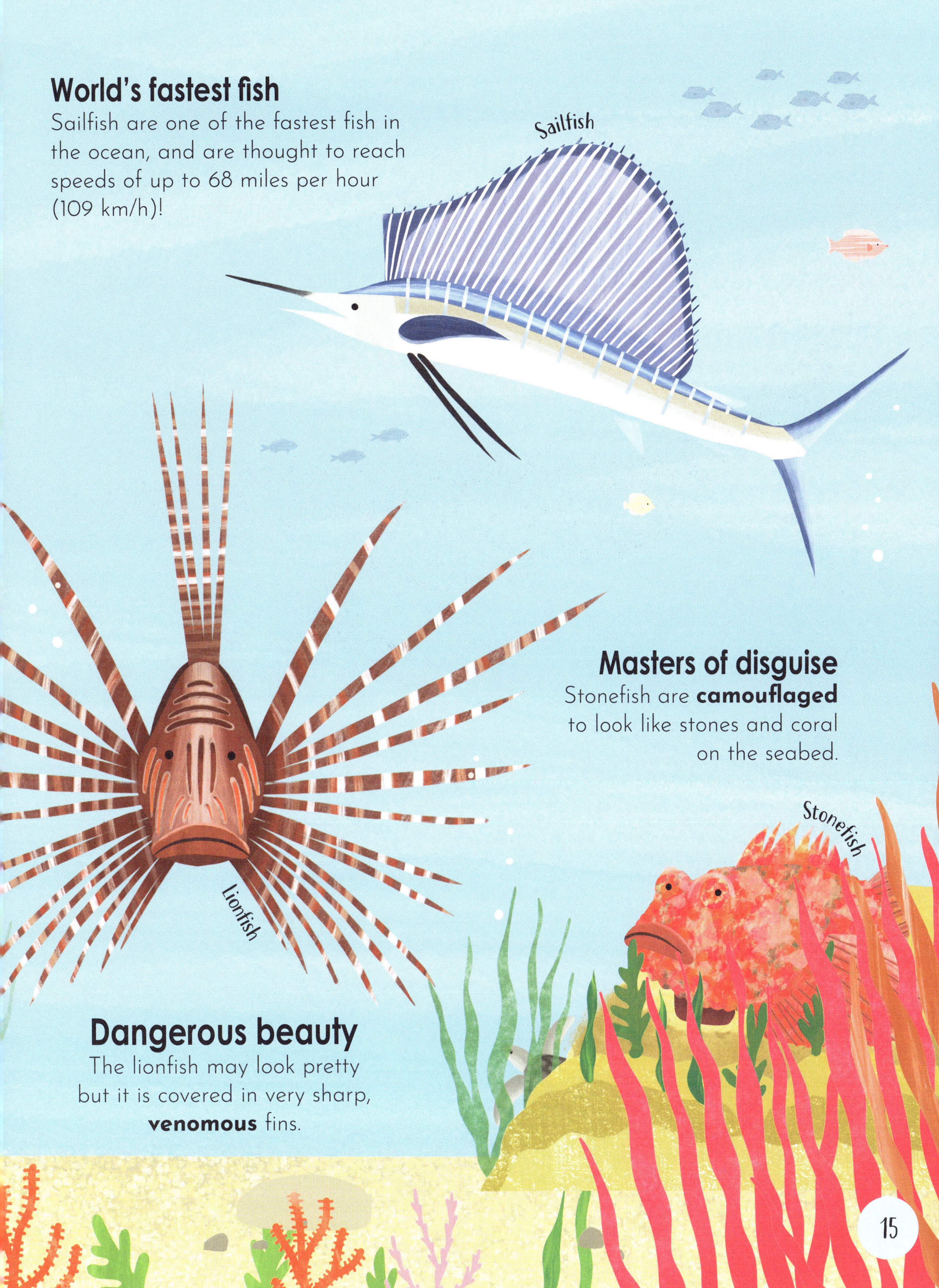

Masters of disguise

Stonefish are **camouflaged** to look like stones and coral on the seabed.

Dangerous beauty

The lionfish may look pretty but it is covered in very sharp, **venomous** fins.

MARINE MAMMALS

It's not just fish in the oceans and seas, there are plenty of mammals too! Mammals don't have gills, so they have to come to the surface of the water to breathe.

Songs of the sea

Humpback whales are famous for singing songs to each other.

The biggest ever!

The blue whale is the largest known animal to have ever existed! They can weigh as much as 40 African elephants!

On land and on sea

Unlike whales and dolphins, seals can live on land too.

Sticking together

Dolphins travel together in groups called pods.

Sea cows

Baby manatees, known as calves, will stay close to their mothers for up to two years.

I SEE SHELLS!

Where do seashells come from? Our oceans and seas of course! Lots of creatures have shells. Here are some for you to spot.

Lots of legs

All crabs have 10 legs. Their front legs have claws, which they use to fight with and catch their food.

Would you hide inside?

Giant clam shells are often big enough that you could fit inside them!

A living fossil

Nautiluses were living in the sea 265 million years before dinosaurs existed! That makes them living **fossils**!

Hidden chompers

Did you know a lobster's teeth aren't in its mouth? They are in its stomach!

Lobster

Plenty of snails

Many seashells you'll find on the beach will have belonged to sea snails. They come in lots of different patterns, shapes, and sizes.

Sea snail

BUT IS IT A FISH?

Sometimes things are not what they seem and names can be misleading. Can you tell which of these creatures are fish and which are something else?

Slip and slide

Eels may look more like snakes but they are a type of fish.

Moray eel

Super stars

Despite their name, starfish are not actually fish. They are related to sea urchins.

Starfish

Jiggling jellies

These strange and beautiful creatures are not fish. They are related to coral and sea anemones.

Horsing around

You may not think it, but seahorses are fish. They are definitely not horses!

Eight-legged brainbox

Octopuses are highly intelligent beings, but they are not fish. They have more in common with slugs and snails.

MONSTERS OF THE DEEP

In the deepest, darkest parts of the ocean live some of the scariest and strangest sea creatures of all!

Eyes up!

This weird looking fish has a see-through head! Its eyes are actually on the inside of its head.

Eyes

Caped creature

The vampire squid isn't really a squid... or a vampire! They are related to octopuses and have eight arms connected to their "cape".

Vampire squid

Nightmare fish

With their giant fangs, these fish may look terrifying, but they are quite small and harmless to humans.

Fangtooth

Long-nosed chimaera

Boo!

These spooky fish are also known as ghost sharks.

Night fishing

This freaky fish has a glowing rod that sticks out of its head to attract **prey**.

Deep sea anglerfish

IN THE DESERT

There is so much to see in these dry and thirsty places. Can you spot the animals and plants that make their home in the desert?

MAJESTIC BEASTS

These large animals have all adapted to survive a long time without water.

Bactrian camels have two humps.

Bactrian camel

Got the hump?

Camels can survive for up to 15 days without drinking. They store fat in their humps which helps them go longer without water.

Dromedaries only have one hump.

Dromedary/Arabian camel

Baby camels are called calves.

A rare sight

The addax is **endangered**. There are only a few left living in the wild.

Long distance hikers

In the desert, elephants will walk up to 50 miles (80 km) a day in search of food.

KEEPING IT COOL

Reptiles are cold-blooded, which means they can't control their body temperature. Most of them spend a lot of time in burrows to try to keep cool.

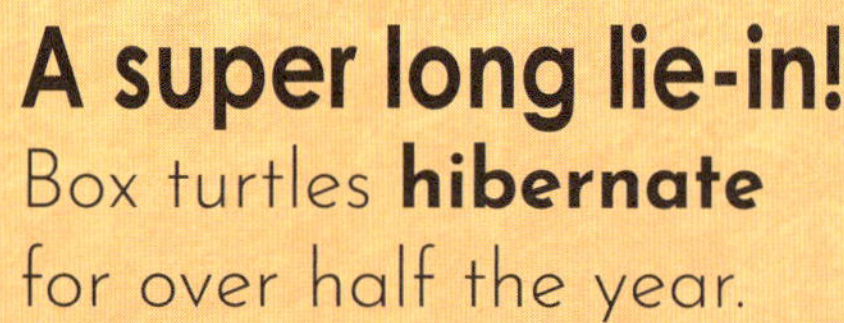

A super long lie-in!

Box turtles **hibernate** for over half the year.

Rattlesnake

Shaking off danger

Rattlesnakes use their rattles to make loud noises to scare off predators.

Mighty monsters

These are the largest lizards living in the United States.

Thirsty?

Desert tortoises can survive a whole year without drinking any water!

Desert devil

This strange looking creature is covered in spikes to help protect itself.

FEATHERED FRIENDS

Take a look at these amazing desert birds! They all live and act in very different ways.

Clever nesting

Gila woodpeckers often make their homes in cacti.

World's largest bird

Ostriches can grow up to 9 feet (2.7 m) tall.

Tasty leftovers

Vultures are **scavengers**, which means they eat animals that are already dead.

Lappet-faced vulture

Night owls

Great horned owls are **nocturnal**. They sleep in the day and hunt at night.

Great horned owl

Kicking up dust

Roadrunners are super speedy and can run up to 27 miles per hour (43 km/h).

Roadrunner

SMALL BUT MIGHTY

These desert creepy-crawlies all have unique skills to help them survive in difficult conditions.

Camel spider

Big biters

Camel spiders use their scary jaws to attack bigger prey, including lizards, snakes and birds!

Dung beetle

Poo pushers

Dung beetles feed on the poo of other animals. Yuck! Some of them roll dung into balls, like this one.

Greedy guzzlers

Locusts can form enormous swarms and travel huge distances, eating every plant in their path.

A sting in the tail

Scorpions use the venomous sting at the end of their tails to hunt their prey.

Quick silver

These ants are covered in shiny hairs that reflect the sun, helping to keep them cool. They are also the fastest ants in the world!

BRILLIANT BURROWERS

It's cool to hang out underground! Many animals escape the heat of the desert by digging burrows to live in.

This meerkat is on guard duty, looking out for predators.

Meerkat

Pack members

Meerkats live together in groups called packs. They all share jobs between them.

Bilby

Burrow for one

Bilbies like their space. They usually live alone and will have up to 12 burrows each!

Sand squatters

These owls like to take over burrows made by other animals.

The better to hear with

These big ears are great for listening out for prey.

Feisty felines

Sand cats may look like cute pets, but they are tough enough to handle extreme desert conditions.

GROWING GETS TOUGH

Most plants need lots of water to grow, but these ones don't mind dry weather.

Clever cacti

Cacti come in lots of different shapes and sizes. They store water in their stems and are covered in sharp spines.

Pretty but prickly

This funny looking cactus produces pretty flowers and edible fruit.

It's a date!

Date palms grow small fruits called dates that have been eaten by humans for many years.

Putting down roots

Joshua trees have very deep roots to reach water hidden underground.

Getting sappy

Agave have sweet sap inside their thick leaves.

Precious treasure

Not many types of flower grow in the desert.

MIGHTY MAMMALS

These mammals are all tough enough to stand the heat of the desert.

Look behind you!

Mountain lions like to sneak up on their prey, often jumping down on them from above.

Butting heads

Male bighorns will use their large, curly horns to fight each other, to prove who is strongest.

Rare runners

These rare gazelles are very good runners. They can reach speeds of 50 miles per hour (80 km/h).

Smells like dinner!

Coyotes have a great sense of smell to help them sniff out food from a long way away.

Big bouncers

Kangaroos don't walk, they jump! They have strong back legs to help them bounce over long distances.

IN THE POLAR REGIONS

The polar regions are the coldest places on Earth! Can you spot the animals that make these freezing lands their home?

THE ANTARCTIC

COOL PENGUINS

Lots of different types of penguin can be found in the Antarctic. They are birds but they can't fly. Their wings act more like flippers.

Wobbly walkers

On land, penguins get around by waddling, jumping and sliding on their bellies.

Flying in water

Penguins are excellent swimmers and spend over half of their time in the water, where they hunt for food.

Proud parents

Mothers and fathers share parenting duties.

Babysitting

Male emperor penguins look after eggs until they hatch.

Love birds

Penguins are very sociable animals. They live in large groups and form couples to **breed** and raise chicks.

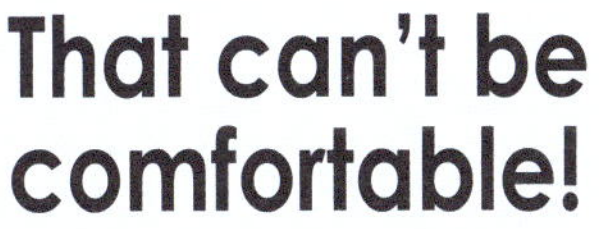

That can't be comfortable!

Some penguins build nests using rocks.

UNDER THE ICE

These sea animals all have blubber, a thick layer of fat under their skin, which helps to keep them warm in the freezing water.

All grown up

Beluga whales only turn white when they become adults.

Curious creatures

Minke whales are very nosey. They will often approach boats in the water to see what's going on.

Unicorns of the sea

The narwhal's famous "horn" is actually an overgrown tooth. No one knows for certain what it's for.

Team players

Killer whales work together in groups called pods to gang up on their prey, like penguins and seals.

BRILLIANT BEARS

Polar bears are specially adapted to living in the Arctic, but it isn't always easy for them. They spend most of their time searching for food, which can be very hard to find.

See-through fur

Their fur may look white, but it's actually **transparent!** Light bounces off it, making the bear look white, and helping them to blend in with the snow.

A playful pair

Polar bear mothers usually give birth to twins. Cubs stay with their mother for just over two years.

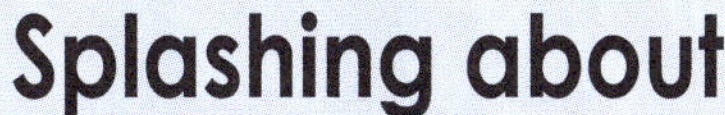

Splashing about

Polar bears are good swimmers. They use their giant front paws like paddles.

What's for dinner?

Polar bears are **carnivores**, which means they mostly eat meat. They like to eat seals a lot!

JOIN THE PACK

Arctic wolves live in groups called packs. There are normally 5-8 wolves in a pack, and they work together as a team when they go hunting.

A varied diet

Arctic wolves are carnivores. They mostly hunt musk oxen and caribou (reindeer) but will also eat seals and other smaller animals and birds.

Sensational senses

Wolves have great eyesight, hearing, and sense of smell, to help them track down food.

Follow the leader

The leader of the pack is known as the Alpha. He is the strongest male in the group.

Wrapped up warm

They have two thick layers of fur to help keep warm. The outer layer is completely waterproof.

FROZEN FLIPPERS

These flippered friends all belong to a family of animals called pinnipeds, which includes seals, sea lions and walruses.

Big seal, big nose

Elephant seals are the largest type of seal. Males have strange, trunk-like snouts.

Long in the tooth

A walrus's tusks continue to grow throughout its life. A male's can reach just over 3 feet (90 cm) in length.

Flipper footed

Instead of feet, seals have two back flippers. These are great for swimming, but not for walking!

Hide-and-go-seek

This pup's fluffy white fur is perfect camouflage against the snow. It will help to keep it hidden from predators until it learns to swim.

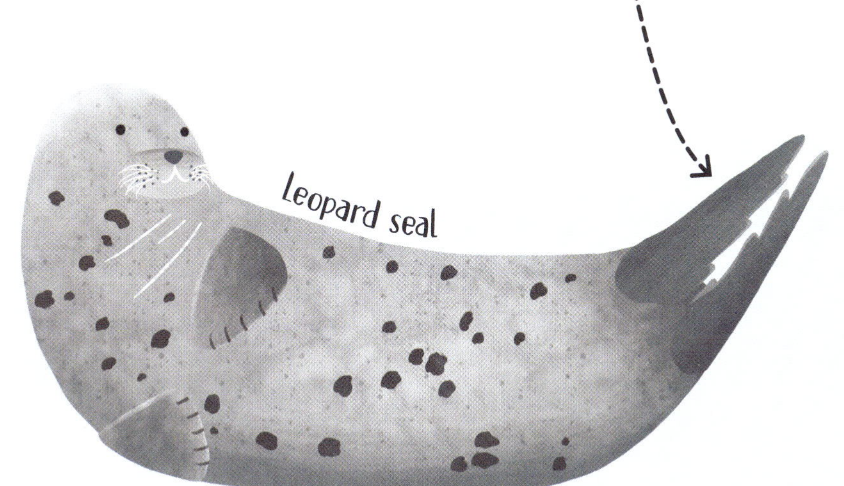

Deep breath!

Seals can hold their breath underwater for up to two hours!

FEATHERED FRIENDS

Some birds, like the snowy owl, don't mind the cold, but others will fly away to warmer places for the winter. This is called migration.

Changing feathers

Ptarmigans lose their feathers twice a year. They are white in the winter and brown in the summer.

Rock ptarmigan

Snowy owl

Sensing in the snow

Snowy owls have excellent eyesight and hearing to help them find their prey in the snow.

From pole to pole

Every year, the Arctic tern travels all the way from the Arctic to the Antarctic Circle and back again - the longest migration in the world!

Stop thief!

The sneaky Arctic skua will often steal food from other birds in mid-air.

Arctic tern

Deep divers

Not only can puffins fly, they can also swim! They will dive underwater up to 200 feet (60 m), in search of fish to eat.

LIFE IN THE TUNDRA

Tundras are large open areas of frozen land where hardly anything grows. These animals have special features to help them survive there.

Wooly beasts

The musk ox has a very long, shaggy woolen coat to help it keep warm in the freezing winters.

Arctic hare

Snow hoppers

Arctic hares have long back feet and strong legs to help them move quickly in the snow.

Caribou (reindeer)

Dashing through the snow

Caribou have large, two-toed hooves, which help them travel easily across snow and are useful for digging through ice to find food.

Fluffy feet

Arctic foxes have fur on the bottom of their feet to protect them from the cold snow and ice.

IN THE RAINFOREST

There is so much to see in the rainforest! Can you spot the amazing animals and plants that make their homes here?

RADIANT REPTILES

Rainforests are warm and wet, which makes them the perfect habitat for lots of different reptiles.

A sixth sense

These snakes have special sensors that allow them to "see" heat. This helps them hunt live prey.

Fancy a change?

Some chameleons can change the patterns on their body. They do this for camouflage and to communicate with others.

Tree huggers

These large snakes live high up in the trees and wrap themselves around branches.

Sticking around

Geckos have lots of tiny hairs on the bottoms of their feet, which help them grip onto branches.

Getting defensive

Iguanas are large lizards with powerful tails and sharp teeth, but they are actually harmless **herbivores**.

GOING APE

Apes are our closest relatives in the animal kingdom. Sadly, all of these apes are endangered because of habitat destruction and poaching.

Going silver

The hair on a male gorilla's back turns silver as it gets older, giving them the name silverback.

Leading the troops

Gorillas are **sociable** and live in groups known as troops, led by the strongest male silverback.

Swinging in the trees
Orangutans have very long, strong arms, which are great for swinging from branch to branch.
Baby bonding
Baby orangutans stay with their mothers for up to 7 years.
Orangutans
We are family
We are most closely related to chimpanzees. They are very intelligent and can make and use tools.
Chimpanzee

BRILLIANT BIRDS

There are lots of beautiful, exotic birds that fly among the tropical treetops.

Close couples

Macaws are parrots that **mate** for life. They form strong bonds and look after their young together.

Blow your horn

This unusual horn is hollow and makes the bird's call much louder, a bit like a trumpet.

Powerful hunters

These massive **birds of prey** have a **wingspan** that can reach over 7 feet (2 m)!

Toucy fruity

A toucan's large, bright beak (or bill) is a useful tool for peeling fruit.

Whirring wings

A hummingbird's wings can beat about 70 times per second, making a humming noise.

PLANT PARADISE

Rainforests are some of the greenest places on Earth, and are home to thousands of different trees and plants.

Twists and twirls

There are more than 2,500 different types of vine that grow in rainforests. They wrap around and hang from trees.

Don't worry, this frog is not being eaten! It is waiting for some tasty insects to come by.

Meat-eating plant

Pitcher plants are carnivorous, which means they eat animals. They trap insects inside their bowl-like pitcher.

Fruits of the forest?

Banana plants look like trees but they are actually giant herbs!

A tasty tree

The pods on this cocoa tree are filled with beans that are used to make chocolate. Yum!

Blooming beautiful

Rainforests contain over 10,000 different kinds of orchid.

HANGING AROUND

Do you like climbing trees? These animals spend lots of time hanging out in their branches.

Laidback life

Sloths are the slowest mammals on the planet and spend most of their life hanging upside down.

Jungle piggyback

Squirrel monkeys carry their babies on their backs as they travel through the trees.

Loud mouth

Howler monkeys live high up in the trees and make deep, loud calls that can be heard up to a mile away!

A balancing act

These lemurs are excellent climbers and use their stripy tails to help them balance.

Head rush

Flying foxes sleep upside down with their wings wrapped around their bodies.

AMAZING MAMMALS

These large, four-legged mammals all make their homes on the forest floor, but tigers, jaguars, and anteaters can climb trees too!

Tiger print

Just like fingerprints, every tiger's stripes are different.

Tip-top tongue

Anteaters use their long tongues to slurp up about 35,000 ants and termites a day!

Jungle athletes

Jaguars are good at both climbing and swimming.

Why the long face?

A tapir's flexible trunk is perfect for stripping leaves off branches.

World's largest rodent

Capybaras look a bit like giant guinea pigs, and they are actually closely related.

LIFE AMONG THE LEAVES

It could be easy to overlook some of the incredible creepy-crawlies hiding in the forest.

Elephant beetle

Brilliant beetles

The male elephant beetle's horns are used as protection from predators and to compete with other males.

Praying mantis

Spikey catchers

Praying mantises have sharp spikes on their front legs to help them catch and kill other insects.

Leaf choppers

These ants have large jaws for cutting up pieces of leaf to carry back home.

Big, blue and beautiful

This stunning butterfly is one of the largest in the world, with a wingspan of 5-8 inches (13-20 cm).

King of the spiders

This tarantula is the biggest spider on the planet! It is large enough to eat small birds, but it usually eats insects.

HABITATS OF THE WORLD

The world is made up of lots of different habitats, with particular plants and animals living in each one. This book only shows a few of these amazing places.

Oceans and seas cover most of the surface of the Earth. Because of their depth, they are the largest habitat of all.

More different types of animals and plants live in the Amazon Rainforest, in South America, than anywhere else in the world!

The world's hot deserts are getting hotter and drier. They are also getting bigger and starting to take up more space on Earth due to global warming.

The polar regions stretch across the very top and very bottom of our planet. It's so cold and icy that trees can't grow there!

Some animals can live in more than one habitat! They migrate between habitats in search of a mate, food, water, and to find better weather.

WHO WAS HIDING?

Did you spot these animals playing hide-and-go-seek throughout the book?

Kemp's Ridley Sea Turtle

This is the smallest type of sea turtle in the world.

I like to eat crab.

Couldn't find him in the deep sea on pages 22-23? It is much too deep and dark for turtles down there!

Egyptian Tortoise

These tortoises live in desert areas in Egypt and Libya in North Africa.

You would have a hard time finding these little creatures in real life. Although many are kept as pets, they are almost **extinct** in the wild.

I prefer to live on my own.

Lemming

Lemmings are small rodents that can be found in the Arctic. They measure between 5-7 inches (13-18 cm).

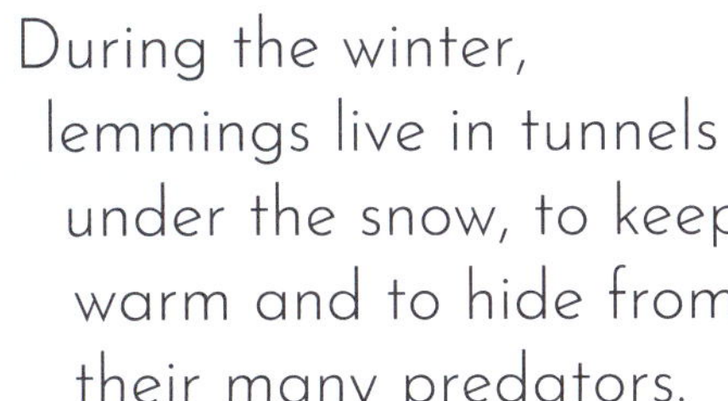

During the winter, lemmings live in tunnels under the snow, to keep warm and to hide from their many predators.

Poison Dart Frogs

These tiny frogs can be found in rainforests in Central and South America.

They are one of the most poisonous animals in the world. Just one lick could be fatal.

Don't eat me! I'm very poisonous.

GLOSSARY

adapted (adaptation) – when a living thing has become able to survive in its surroundings by developing special features or skills over a long period of time.

birds of prey – birds that mainly eat meat.

blubber – a special layer of fat under the skin that keeps animals warm.

breed – to make babies.

burrow – a tunnel or hole in the ground made by an animal.

camouflage - to look like something else so as not to be easily seen.

carnivores (carnivorous) - animals (or plants!) that mainly eat meat.

cold-blooded – animals with bodies that do not produce their own heat, and have to be heated or cooled by their surroundings.

endangered – if a type of animal or plant is in danger of dying out forever, then they are known as endangered.

extinct – when a type of plant or animal no longer exists anywhere in the world.

fossils - the remains or traces of plants and animals that lived a very long time ago.

gills – a body part that fish and some other animals use to breathe underwater.

habitat – where an animal or plant lives.

herbivores – animals that only eat plants.

hibernate – animals that hibernate spend their time sleeping during the winter and only wake up when it's warm again.

immune – to be protected from/unaffected by something, such as an illness or a poison.

inflate – to make larger.

mammals – animals with specific features. They all have hair or fur, drink milk from their mothers as babies, have a backbone and are **warm-blooded** (they can keep their bodies warm, even when it's cold outside). Humans are mammals too!

mate – when animals form a pair that they have babies with.

migration – to travel from one place to another at different times of year.

nocturnal – animals that sleep in the day and come out at night-time.

poaching – illegal hunting of animals by humans.

predators – animals that hunt and kill other animals for food.

prey – an animal that is hunted by other animals for food.

reptiles – are animals with specific features. Reptiles have dry skin with scales, a backbone, breathe using lungs and are cold-blooded (see left).

scavengers – scavengers don't hunt live animals. They eat animals that are already dead.

sociable – animals and people that are friendly and like spending time with others.

transparent - clear or see-through, like glass.

venomous – poisonous, or containing poison.

wingspan – the distance from the tip of one wing to the other when they are fully stretched out.